TIME to WAKE UP:

SAVE MONEY and

GET OUT of DEBT

Lawrence Burns

Disclaimer

The material in this publication is of the nature of general comment only, and does not represent professional advice. It is not intended to provide specific guidance for particular circumstances and it should not be relied on as the basis for any decision to take action or not take action on any matter which it covers. Readers should obtain professional advice where appropriate, before making any such decision. Therefore, if you wish to apply ideas contained in this book, you are taking full responsibility for your actions. To the maximum extent permitted by law, the author and publisher disclaim all responsibility and liability to any person, arising directly or indirectly from any person taking or not taking action based upon the information in this publication.

ISBN-13: 978-1492324263
ISBN-10: 1492324264

DEDICATION

This book is dedicated to my loving family:

To the mothers Iris and Ninelia who mastered all skills and creative ways to create something out of nothing. I salute you both. Thank you for always being here and for teaching love and respect.

To my dear wife Marina who lights up my life, I love you.

To the children Stephen, Alison, Ekaterina and Daria whom I love equally and who always kept me on my toes.

To my grandfather Lawrence and to Cyril, sole maternal uncle, who both died as a result of war service, protecting family and country. I wish I had known you better.

To my family's elders, Lawrence, Mary, Ellen, Felix, Bob, Nick & Ritson who influenced and shaped my young life. Thanks for teaching me there is no such word as can't and that if you don't aim for anything, you won't hit it.

To my other family members Eva, Carole and their children and children's children who are the living proof, that creativity in any of its forms is a strong genetic force. Collectively we are artists, musicians writers, craftsmen, poets, teachers, culinary artists and more. You are perfect just the way you are.

CONTENTS

CONTENTS

ACKNOWLEDGMENTS

I would like to acknowledge my friends John and Dot Wakeling, Ray and Shirley Kilner, Cyril Ridley, Moana, and Graeme Woods & family. Thank you all for the hundreds of years of collective friendship, good humour, whacky jokes and just being there for me throughout. I love you all. Thanks for being part of my life.

x

PREFACE

This book is written to benefit all people doing it tough for whatever the reason. It doesn't matter whether you are pensioners trying to eke out your pension or you are a single living alone, a family, or a single parent. You are the only one who can save your money. Improving your financial situation is not rocket science. Just think carefully and stick to the money saving ideas. Success is not only possible; it is guaranteed and is based on your level of determination. I hear you asking, "How can you say this?" The answer is, "I know what I am talking about, I have done it all, and reached all my goals". The content is not just a bunch of words written by an individual who read them somewhere and has never known what "to want" really is. This book is based on personal real life experiences which have been tried and tested over a very long period of time.

My experiences of the entire spectrum of life are: from being a single and living alone, to a financially challenged family man, a solo parent, an unemployed family man, and finally becoming both a disabled and an age pensioner. The journey has been amazing on so many levels. Now I hope to share with you some of the discoveries that can help you improve your quality of life.

The road has often been painful but gave me a wealth of knowledge. Many mistakes were made; however, you can limit your pain by benefiting from my experiences. At the end of the day, I have my own fully owned home, a nice car and there is very little else in life I want or need apart from good friends and good health but no amount of money will buy either of them. So you see, no matter how tough it is or how dark it seems right now, there is always a silver lining as anything is possible if you apply yourself.

In reading on, do not expect that every element discussed under the following headings will apply to your situation. It won't, and the reason for that is because this is not an individual plan for you personally based on in depth discussion and an individual analysis of your situation.

The content is written for the larger audience attempting to bring to all readers the maximum amount of helpful hints for saving money from your budget, therefore, allowing you to either save, or to use those monies in other areas.

I am totally unbiased: none of the websites/ software/ books offered in this book were selected in order to be compensated by their authors for promotions of their products.

INTRODUCTION

We live in unusual times, in a society of high technology, of mass communications and of plastic money. We have for the first time ever manufacturing processes which have resulted in some prices falling by around 50% per annum while the product's capabilities actually doubles. Online buying is escalating at a huge rate giving everyone the options of buying in a global marketplace. It's very easy to get a credit card (in fact several) and to overspend your limit on each of them. Banks constantly press you to increase your credit limit rather than to behave responsibly and show you how to set up and operate a family budget. They won't tell you that by saying the right things and pressing the right people's buttons you can reduce your credit card interest rate by as much as 22 percent. THINK ABOUT THAT A MOMENT.

In my younger days you couldn't get finance from banks and financial institutions until you were aged 21 and in full-time employment, not for a home, not for a car, not for anything. Today we have banks and financial institutions giving $20,000 plus loans to seventeen year olds who work one day a week and for a V8 car they can't even afford to fill with fuel. No other wonder there is so much bankruptcy. The reality of today is that savvy fourteen year olds can also be multi millionaires through, for instance, some form of online activity such as blogging, youtubing, program development, and other monetization sources from the "information super highway".

One of the greatest objectives you can ever set for yourself is to "cut up the plastic" and release yourself from the bond of high credit card debt and interest repayments.

Saving money does not mean you have to skimp continually and to put yourself in depression just to buy cheaper goods. Saving is something entirely different; it is the art of minimizing wasteful or unnecessary spending.

Economy is not a compromise in the quality of things. It is to buy items of the same quality at a lower cost price than you planned or originally expected. Savings should be rational and reasonable. If you were to economize on buying fruits and vegetables, for example, family health problems could result and create much greater cost/ troubles (doctors/ medical bills) down the line. On the other hand, if you purchased reduced price jeans on sale at a fashion store (and such events are held regularly), then you are buying quality jeans at a lower price. You save without reduction in quality and so benefit both ways.

Buying cheaper things do not necessarily lead to the desired savings and I am not advocating 'buying cheap'. What I am advocating is to be wise and think before you buy. You can then write down every dollar you saved, enjoying each little victory as you watch your savings grow. (See My Financial Victory List at the end of the book).

1 MANAGING MONEY IS NOT EASY

Sometimes, when you look at your bank statement and see a smaller balance than you thought, you may ask, where did the money go? Often it is very difficult to remember what the missing money was spent on. In a matter of cash withdrawals, this is even more evident as there will not always be receipts for what you spent it on.

In order to be financially free, remember, that when you set a budget, your "Outgoings" (what you spend) should never be greater than your "Income" (what you earn). An "Income" of $100 versus "Expenses" of $120 results in a negative cash flow, which is counter productive. With an "Income" of $100 and "Expenditure" of $80 the result is both, satisfactory and productive.

It has been widely suggested that obesity comes from junk eating. As a matter of fact, gaining weight comes from "junk thinking". Inability to save money comes from "junk thinking", too. Some people would think about saving money as being miserable, greedy, depriving themselves of all things they like to do and hoarding for "rainy days". In reality, saving money is fun. It is a game with your own rules.

The trick is to set your mind towards placing your finances under control and to start saving money. Nobody can do it for you except yourself.

Let's compare saving money with losing weight:

	Losing weight	Saving money
You can talk to many different:	Dieticians, weight loss specialists	Financial advisors, Debt Assistance experts
You can purchase:	Gym equipment, gym membership	Financial software, debt/ saving money calculators
You can search for:	Different diet pills, diet plans	Latest trends in saving money

(and I am not saying you don't need all the above)

The main issue is:	Calories eaten is greater than calories burned	Money spent is greater than money owned

In order to succeed:

Who needs to face the issue?	**You do**
Who must fully believe in your capability to deal with the issue?	**You do**
Who must take steps and actually do it?	**You do**

As much as it is important to change your eating and exercise patterns in losing weight, the most important factor in saving money is to change your spending habits.

Planning and commitment are two key factors in achieving a successful outcome. For every project we need a road map: a business plan for a new business, a to-do list for managing everyday tasks and getting things done, a diet/ workout plan for losing weight and a budget to save money.

Managing on a Low Income Is Tough

There is a fairly widespread belief that saving money can only be accomplished by people with high level earnings. This is the most misleading myth. In order to have a sufficient amount of money for living, you need to either increase your income or reduce costs. If the first option is unobtainable, think about the second. It is not easy, but to achieve this you might have to change some habits. If you smoke (I wouldn't tell you how bad it is for you), you might come to the decision to stop smoking by yourself, regardless of either saving money or improving your health. Even if you are not ready to stop smoking, you could just reduce the amount of cigarettes you smoke. If you save $10 a week on smoking, the saving comes to $520 a year. I can't put this figure into my Financial Victory List because I stopped smoking more than 30 years ago (wow, I have saved a lot of money taking into account that I smoked at least 20 cigarettes a day!).

Saving $3 to $4 on 1 cup of coffee by having a glass of water instead will save another $1095 a year (3$ x 365 = $1095) or $1460 if you paid $4 a cup.

Many people on low income ask the same question, "Why to bother to count pennies?" The simple answer is, "It is better to have the penny in your pocket than in somebody else's".

Collectively we love discussing income of celebrities and say, "Oh, well, they are rich, they can afford it". Have you ever thought why they are rich? Many of them have gone through years and years of study, sleepless nights, memorizing formulas or the name of each bone in a human body. A percentage of them have incredible talents (but they still work very hard in order to be rich) especially those in age limited careers like athletes, footballers etc. What all wealthy people have in common (here I refer to millionaires who created their own wealth) is that they all manage their money. It really doesn't matter if you have a low or high income; you still have to manage your money. You need to take responsibility for your financial future and become the managing director of your own financial department. Being the manager means to comply with the rules and to maintain financial discipline. So, you have a new job now and your salary is your saving, the more you save the more you have.

A penny saved is a penny earned.

Before we get into the various elements of improving the quality of your life and discuss how you can save money, I want to share with you a few thoughts which will also help you from this moment on.

A Shower for the Soul

Have you ever wondered why some people try to play musical instruments without a music sheet or harmonic knowledge and only hear discordant sound? I am not a good piano player; have never had a piano lesson and don't know how to properly place my fingers on the keys. I sit and execute what passes for my version of playing piano, which is mostly when I am feeling very stressed, angry, sad or unhappy. The piano becomes my best friend and magic happens. It listens to me without any words. I feel like my entire pain, stress or unhappiness passes away from me like waves, through my fingers into the piano keys. After some time I get up and I feel calmer. My soul is peaceful and feels like it had a shower and all the negative energy is gone from me. Hope you don't live next door, hahaha.

People do different things to deal with frustration: painting, drawing, doodling (an unfocused drawing) or knitting and all sorts of hobbies. I am not trying to advise you in this book how to control your anger or get out of depression. When you plan your money, debts, liabilities, budget, it is better to take a paper (dedicated notebook is even better) and a pen and start writing all of your figures down. There is something very positive about the act of committing to paper. It's up to you whether or not you use financial/ budgeting software. There are plenty of financial/ budgeting software programs and spreadsheets (see 'Comparison of spreadsheet software' at **http://tinyurl.com/2c4a6k**) exist today for PCs, Macs, tablets and phones. My belief is that when you see your budget written by your own hand, you are more likely to commit to it and achieve better results. Using a new software program can be frustrating due to lack of familiarity. Sometimes, when you start to use a new software program, your thoughts move away from what you are actually doing. When you write all figures down, the negativity and frustration may flow from your mind and will go through your fingers, through your pen and onto the paper. With the budgeting job done, you will relax and your soul will become quiet. You will feel calmer, just like you do after a long, warm shower.

Denial Is Not a River in Europe

Many people don't want to admit that they need help with financial management in order to be free from debt. Denial is a defense mechanism to cover up budgetary weakness or inability to save. Financial problems will not disappear by themselves and things can go from bad to worse. The good news is that if you are reading books on saving money, you are on a way to control your finances and your future.

Some people are sure that they will fail at whatever they do because they are lacking in confidence. Everyone occasionally fails to meet their goals. There is no shame in failing. Shame comes from being unwilling to try again. All you need to do is pick yourself up, dust yourself off, and try all over again. Only losers give up. I believe that in every bad experience we have there is a lesson, a diamond. All we need to do is to look at what has occurred and find the diamond.

Once you have found it, you will never repeat the same mistake again.

Set Goals and Stop Putting Money Down the Drain

You need to be able to measure your progress therefore goal setting will be your yardstick. Use a Task List. The Task List or To Do List is a great tool; it really helps to make a daily list of everything you want to achieve. Not only will you find you will actually accomplish more every day but you will surprise yourself by finding it can be a fun. I remember many experiences of joy when I actually accomplished projects I had been putting off for so long because I told myself they would be both time consuming and difficult. Afterwards came the feeling of bewilderment wondering why I had built the task up in my mind as such a huge problem. Generally speaking, as humans we tend to over complicate things and often ignore the obvious yet simple solution because we refuse to believe that it is simply 'that easy'. The other valuable aspect of using a List is that you can re prioritize quickly when matters, over which you have limited or no control, come into play.

The goal is what you are trying to accomplish. The goal should be clear, be specific and you need to believe in it. Our goals here are to become money wise, to develop good financial management skills, to be free of debt and to be on the path to financial well-being. Now we need to have a look at all strategies and the tools to achieve our goals:

1. To master the skills of preparation the family budget.

2. Practice saving skills. (Practice makes perfect!).

3. Count money. Counting money forms a habit; it becomes part of our existence (like brushing the

teeth!).

Action Steps

- Set up your goals and write down your financial targets. It doesn't need to be overcomplicated, but the truth of the matter is that without setting your goals you are like a ship at sea without a compass, you just don't know which direction to go. If you are lucky, you might find a safe port, however, it's more probable you will end up floundering on the rocks. In order to accomplish something you need to decide what to accomplish, set your targets and go for them.

So, the simplest target action plan needs to be set in a following way:

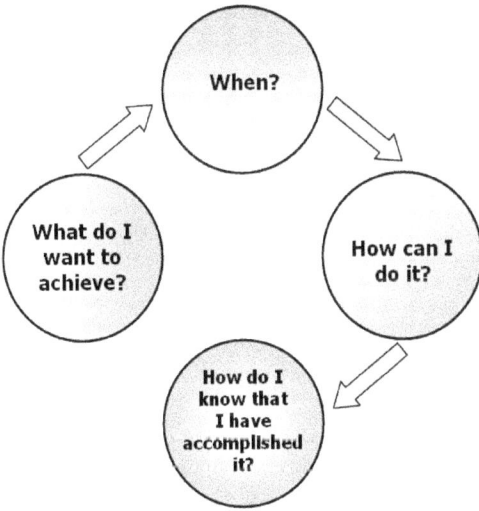

- When you write down your targets and goals you need to mean it and be prepared to work towards to accomplishing your targets.

- It's now time to begin creating your Financial Victory List in order to see how the financial goals are going to be reached and plan how to celebrate your financial winnings. You can see my Financial Victory List in Chapter 5.

2 BUDGET ISO TRIANGLE

Setting a family budget is not really very complicated. Our family budget is a basic ISO (Income, Savings, and Outgoings) Triangle:

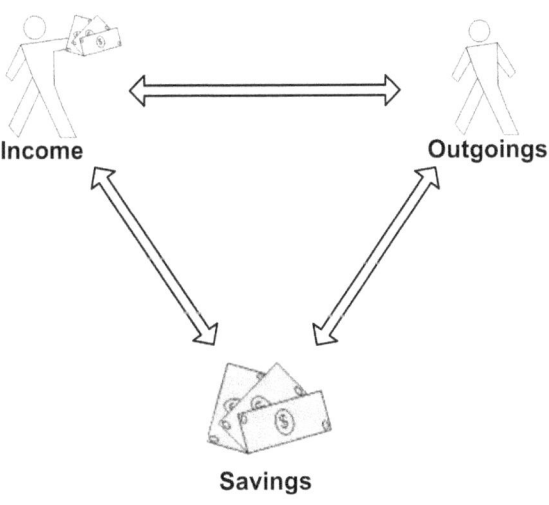

In our own budget Outgoings mostly derive from Income and some of it may come from Savings. Savings mostly grow from Income but may arise from Outgoings (for example, solar panels for generating your energy).

Saving Goals

How to Set and Prioritize Savings Goals?

First, your budget needs to be set and debts have to be paid or be under control. It's not easy to get on this road free of debts (sometimes debts grow like mushrooms after rain). This suggests how you may decide to write down your list of saving   goals:

- Where do I want to be?

- When?

- How will I get there?

- How do I know that I have arrived?

In order to be debts free many people use the popular "debt snowball method" which is based on writing a list of all your debts from lowest to highest balance, to pay towards each debt a minimum amount of money all except for the lowest balance. This is paid the maximum you can until finished. Such will eliminate the lowest debt balance leaving one debt less. By repeating this method the next lowest balance debt will be eliminated and so repeats the story. You can find a good example of the debt-snowball method at Wikipedia (**http://tinyurl.com/4vxzed**).

Second, write down all of the things that you'd like to save for: "Need - How long can it wait" and "Want - How long can it wait"). For example:

I Need	How Long Can It Wait
New vacuum cleaner	Can't wait, consider renting
Exercise bicycle	Can't wait, consider doing exercises at home (hula-hoop?) or gym
A PC tablet (for work after hours)	Can wait until next months, consider to buy pre-loved / refurbished

I Want	How Long Can It Wait
Black shoes	I really want shoes as soon as possible because I can't wear that lovely black dress
New large screen TV	My TV doesn't have a good picture but it can wait a couple of months until Christmas sales
Trip to Egypt	For some time, perhaps even couple of years

The list can go on and you need to prioritize and think about the most important things for you. The more precise you are, the more precise your results can be.

Next, once you know what you want and have prioritized, you can decide how to get it. You can organize different envelopes with signs "New TV" or "Trip to Egypt", etc. and put money in each of them. Snowball method can be applied here too. You can put a bit more money into the "Most Wanted" item on your preference list.

Outgoings

Outgoings (expenditure) are amounts of money that are disbursed for bills and incidentals on a regular basis. The purpose of this book is to find out how we can reduce our

Outgoings in order to increase our Savings. Chapter 3 is fully dedicated to just this matter.

Master the Family Budget

I set my family budget based on ISO triangle and an online budget provided by the Australian Securities and Investments Commission's (ASIC) consumer website MoneySmart (**https://www.moneysmart.gov.au/**):

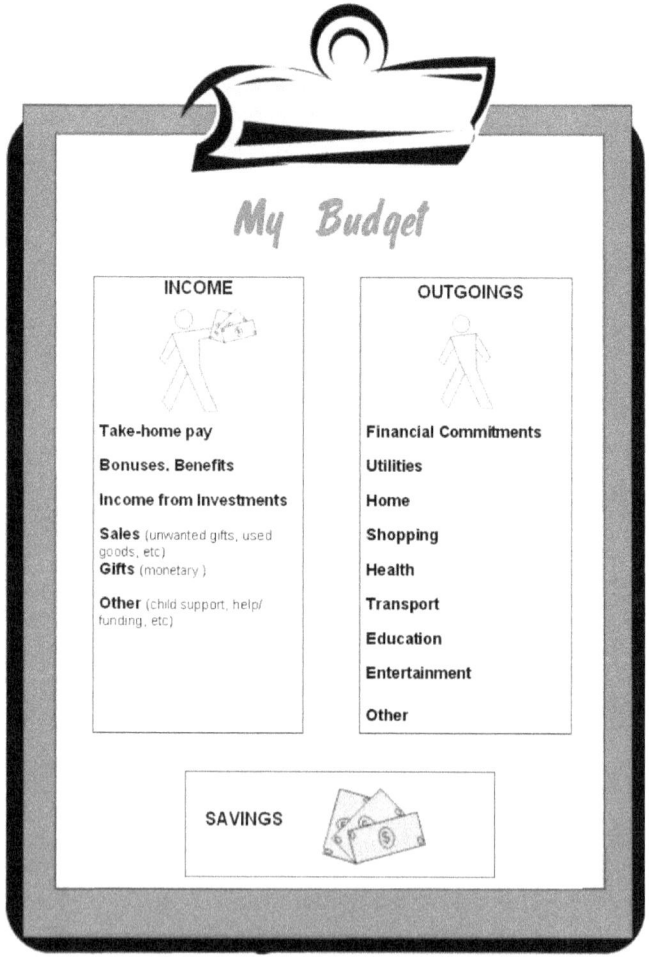

You have noticed that Savings part of the picture doesn't have any source of money written there. This is because the source of saving money is different for every one of us. Mainly, Savings will come from Income but we are going to discuss how to save money which means that our saved money will arise from Outgoings. Let's have a closer look at Outgoings:

- Financial Commitments are our legal duty to pay and we have to meet these liabilities. They mainly are: rent/ mortgage/ land tax/ rates, child support, loan repayments (car, furniture, equipment, etc.), and credit card interests.

- Utilities are services and by definition are everyday necessities: electricity/ gas/ water/ garbage pick-up, internet, phone, paid TV, etc.

- Home expenses or expenses associated with your home usually are: insurance (home, content), maintenance and repair, and new furniture/ appliances.

- Shopping includes food/ fruits/ vegetables, baby products, cleaning products, clothing/ shoes, cosmetics/ toiletries, etc.

- Health expenses are associated with our health such as Private Health insurance, Life insurance/ other insurance (Accident, Funeral, etc.), doctors, prescriptions and other medicine, gym/ sporting memberships.

- Transport expenditure relates to our personal mobility management and usually includes car insurance, fuel, car maintenance, public transport costs/ other transport costs.

- Education costs involve childcare/ pre-school/ school/ college fees, uniform, books, excursions, tutoring, classes (sport, music, dance, etc.), and courses (upskilling).

- Entertainment is our leisure, fun and enjoyable time and expenses include paying for movies/ theater/ shows/ music, newspapers/ magazines, bars/ clubs/ alcohol/ cigarettes, celebrations, hobbies, holidays, eating out (restaurants/ takeaways, bought lunches/ snacks, coffee/ tea/ soft drinks), etc.

- The last outgoings category includes money we spend on gifts, visitors (planned/ unplanned), unplanned meetings/ ceremonies and gambling.

The above nine categories are the subject of our discussion in further chapters.

Action Steps

- Plan to "Snowball" your debts. When you organize your debts in the lowest-balance-first order you will see your progress and it will encourage you and make you more motivated because of your achievement and financial victory!

- Now complete your "I NEED/ I WANT" Lists, prioritize, than, write down "How long can it wait". Can you "Snowball" your wishes and needs? Snowballing will be different here from dealing with debts because you start not from the lowest-cost-first, but most desirable/ needed- first order, the idea is the same.

- Create your own family budget "Income – Outgoings – Savings" and have a look at all the saving possibilities you have.

3 ARE YOU SPENDING MORE THAN YOU CAN AFFORD?

Most people do spend more than they can afford. For many of us it can be a constant struggle living hand to mouth and pay check to pay check. There are plenty of unavoidable expenses in our life, such as rent/ mortgage, child support, bills, medical expenses, emergency expenses and funeral costs, – the list goes on. You can save money even on unavoidable expenses, not to mention avoidable ones. Buying items on credit or finances causes the price of the item to increase by at least the interest rate applied and leads to the accumulation of the debt.

For example, your credit card balance is $3,000.00. Assuming that you make no more charges and pay only the minimum payment of $50.00 each month at the Annual Interest Rate (APR) of 17% , it will take 135 months (about 11 years) to pay off your balance. In that amount of time you will pay $3,744.00 in Interest charges. (*Credit Card Repayment Calculator - **http://tinyurl.com/ 4recul4**).

Increasing your monthly payment to $75.00 a month will

save you $2,285.00 in interest charges. If you pay $100.00 each month (at the same 17% APR) you can pay your debt off in 40 months with total interest of $934.01 (*Calculator - **http://tinyurl.com/ bhgk57v**). Paying $299.00 per months will allow you to pay your credit card balance off in 12 months with total interest of $284.00 and increasing your monthly payment to $349.00 a month will save you $62.00 in interest charges. So, let's have a look at all our calculations (Assuming Credit card balance is $3000.00 and Annual Interest Rate is 17%):

Monthly Repayments, $	Time to pay the debt off, months	Interest you pay, $
50.00	135	3,744.00
75.00	60	1,459.00
100.00	40	934.00
200.00	17	397.00
299.00	12	284.00
349.00	10	222.00

There are definitely things to think about. The actual time and cost to pay off your debt will depend on the terms of your account and future account activity.

The main benefit of having credit cards is the convenience of having what you want now and paying for them later. Buying on credit allows us to have the goods we can't afford to pay for right on the spot. In addition, many credit cards offer rewards and benefits, for example, rental car insurance or travel medical insurance. Credit cards can also offer reward points which may be redeemed for cash or products. Surely, you have to pay back what you borrow by a certain date, plus pay interest.

You need to decide when to use credit and when to use another alternative to get the things you want. For example, consider your choices for a new Apple 32GB iPad:

- Rent it. You would pay $1,973.40 ($37.95 p/week x 52 weeks).

- Buy it on credit. With a 17% interest rate and 12 months to pay it back you would pay $710.28 (monthly payment required $59.19, Interest $61.28).

- Save for it. Save $25 per week and pay cash for the iPad in 26 weeks (6 month). This is the lowest cost alternative - $649.00.

It's rarely better to live on credit. Avoid getting into the habit of having big debts on credit cards. The interest is usually very high, up to 23%. Over a time, debt snowballs and quickly overwhelms you. Debts can destroy families and lives. According to the report, "The Financial Status and Decision-Making of the American Middle Class," by the Consumer Federation of American (CFA) and Primerica, 67 % of middle-class Americans admits to having made a "really bad financial decision" and almost half made more than one (Consumer Federation of America and Primerica, Inc. – Sep 18, 2012 **http://tinyurl.com/d8crn4o**).

So, think carefully before purchase items on credit. The simple rule is, "If you can't afford it, don't buy it". If you really need to buy emergency goods, you might consider taking a bank loan. Interest rates at banks may be between 30 to 50 % lower than the credit card interest rate. If you have a large credit card debt, you might come to a decision to take a bank loan to cover it and so reduce the level of your debt. You just need to think and carefully compare interest rates.

People, who are constantly battling their debt, feel that

they can never catch up with their finances. We have to learn to stop spending what we can't afford. It is hard and easier said than done. I didn't smoke for some time not because I decided to stop smoking (I wish I had!) but because I didn't have money to buy cigarettes. My code in life has always been: paying the bills and looking after the children first, after that any adults needs. Sometimes in my life I had to walk or bike to work because I simply didn't have money for a bus ticket. I had extremely tight budget as a single parent. I was at that point of my life when making more money by being away from the home wasn't the answer. I had to find a way to spend less money. It was a necessity; otherwise, my debts would accumulate in no time. I needed to cut my budget and learn to manage my money better than ever. I looked at every expense closely and had more time to develop my budgeting skills. After slashing expenses from my social life, I started to write down every item where I could possibly save. It only took a couple of months and my debt started to shrink significantly. Money management is a learned skill and I learned the hard way. In the next chapter I want to share my savings tips in the hope they will benefit you, making it easier for you to manage your money.

Salespeople are Not Your Friends

Selling is a psychological game and there is a whole army of professionals working on the subject of "How to sell anything to anyone".

Why do we keep forgetting all the time that salespeople don't worry about our well-being? They only worry about their commissions and pay checks. It is their job to sell and if they would worry about your financial situation or your other issues, they would be battling against their own debt crisis. They are highly skilled at lip service and will tell you what you want to hear. The salesperson tries hard to convince you that he/ she is trying to help you, rather than to make money off you. A salesperson manipulates you to feel what they want you to feel.

You are treated to a dissertation about all benefits of the product but never hear the negative side of the story. Let's say your face moisturizer has 3 years of shelf life. What does it tell you? It tells me that the moisturizer is full of chemical preservatives. Everything you put on your skin will absorb into your blood stream and will affect your health, often in a negative way. There is a warning sign on cigarette packs that smoking can cause cancer. Have you ever seen the same sign on your anti-wrinkle cream? Did the salesperson who sold you this cream tell you about the risk of toxic chemical build-up in your body? I bet not. Salespeople know that you would rather buy a "strawberry pie, that melts in your mouth" than a "frozen fruit dessert". A salesperson's primary goal is to sell you a product, then to up sell additional goods or services. He/ she will always promote self image saying "let's see what I can do for you". They play on your emotions rather than your intellect. I am not saying that a salesperson is a bad person. I am saying that "creative description" comes with the job and if they tell you the truth (sometimes they don't even know what the truth is) they might never make a good living.

A salesperson wants you to believe that buying an item cheaper is a "win" for you. In reality, it is your "win" only if it met your goals. If the item you just negotiated a better price for was in your "Need List", it will be your "win". If the item wasn't your goal, you just let a salesperson to win by using his/ her strategies and tools and you lost.

Spending Diary

Spending Diary could be your best friend. Your spending diary will show you where your money has gone. You can create a table (in writing or using spreadsheet software) and enter all your outgoings as headings with two very important columns in addition: 1. Purchase planned/ unplanned and 2. Should I really buy it?

When you start to analyze your purchases you will learn a lot about your own spending habits and learn money management science from your own mistakes. Believe me, the time you spend on filling out the diary and analyzing your spending patterns will be one of the best things you can do to strengthen your financial position. Again, you are investing in your future.

Action Steps

• Create your spending diary with headings: Financial Commitments, Utilities, Home, Shopping, Health, Transport, Education, Entertainment, Other (unplanned) and learn money management science by analyzing your own spending habits.

• Remember your budget, be firm and learn to say "NO" to salespeople even if a deal sounds very sweet. You don't owe the salesperson anything. Unplanned purchase will generate a new debt for an item you never really wanted.

• Continue to "Snowball" your debts. If you managed to reduce debts - Congratulations! Record your financial Victory and think about your next step to your wealth.

4 TURN THE MONEY MARATHON INTO A WALK IN A PARK

Let's get our gear ready and turn the money marathon into a walk in a park. The money will stop running (away) very quickly if we apply our saving program. Let's call it the Victory Saving Program because if you read this book you already are thinking about your money management skills and you are going to win your financial battle.

Victory Savings Program

When we follow the plan, we are clearly making a decision of where, when and how much we can save.

Let's follow our spending diary with headings.

4.1. Financial Commitments

Rent/ Mortgage/ Land Tax/ Rates

There are a few options you should consider in order to

lower your rent. Some of them might be common sense for you, but it's always good to get a refresher!

- Do your research on price of rent in your neighborhood, surrounding areas. What is the tendency in the rental market? Are there plenty of empty houses/ units around?

- What are mortgage loans interest trends are doing? If mortgage loans interests move up, there will be more families in the renting market.

Based on the results of your research you might make a decision to find another place or negotiate with your landlord for a lower rent. Or you may even put a deposit down to get your own home.

- Consider sharing rent by finding a roommate. Move further from the city / place of work or to a smaller accommodation, offer some energy exchange to your landlord (for lowering rent you can tutor landlord's children in some school subjects, take their dog for a walk, or re-tile their kitchen). It all depends on your individual circumstances and skills but it is always another way to save.

- If you are currently dealing with an agency remember that it may be worth finding a private landlord and dealing directly with him/ her. An agency is a "salesperson" and the higher the rent you pay, the higher the agency commission is. It's about 10-12 %.

- The mortgage can be reduced too. Almost every bank website has Mortgage Reduction Calculator. You have to have a look at the terms of your existing mortgage contract. Refinancing your mortgage might or might not be the best solution for you.

• Owing your own home may be your dream; however you might decide to sell your property to clear your debt. Selling on your terms is always better than having a property repossessed as mortgage lenders sell to protect only their financial interest. They are not there to protect your level of investment, no matter what you think.

Loan Repayments and Credit Cards Interests

Using credit cards has advantages and disadvantages. Credit cards are convenient and allow us to make a purchase even if we don't have the money. A disadvantage is that credit comes at a cost (do you remember our "debt snowball method" discussion and a simple summary - "If you can't afford it, don't buy it"?).

We need to look at lowering debt by negotiating a lower credit interest rate with the credit card providers. By taking out new credit cards with lower interest rates and using them to pay off the higher debt balance on the current cards, you will be saving the percentage difference. It is possible to get rates reduced from as much as 23% all the way down to a low of 0.9% or to some point in between. Search for the best possible rate. Any reduction is a win and all wins are savings which you can add to your Financial Victory List.

The debt will not go away itself so you can't just ignore it. If you can't pay your debt, then you need to do something about it. You can:

• Seek help and talk to a debt-management counselor/ financial advisor to help you to arrange payment plans with creditors.

• Downsize (your spending, paid entertainment, place of living, etc.).

• Consider using public transport (if you don't have a car, you don't have a lot of different bills like registrations, insurances, etc.).

• Sell things you can live without.

• Find another source of income (for example, second job).

• Employ most of the saving tips we are going to discuss in this chapter.

4.2. Utilities

Utilities are an important part of our budget. Without utilities your place of living is just a cave, a roof over your head. There are a plenty of opportunities to save here.

Electricity/ Gas/ Water

With suppliers constantly increasing the cost of electricity (better than 50%) during the last 5 years) this is definitely an area we need to look at.

Switching off lights and appliances when not actually in use (yes, it is a common sense!) is something we hear a lot about but many people choose to ignore it. In business I saved as much as 25 % of my power bill simply by following a plan and shutting off power (lights, etc.) left on by others in empty rooms. Leaving appliances on standby (computers, televisions, Hi Fi systems, etc. can use up to 10% of your total electrical supply so it makes sense to switch them off.

Common cheapest light bulbs (Incandescent lighting) are

the least energy efficient and have a shortest average operating life. Therefore, there is not much saving in buying cheapest light bulbs. According to **http://energy.gov** website, compact fluorescent lamps (CFLs) will save about 75% of electricity and work 10 times longer.

What draws the most power in your home? The answer is: ovens, water heaters, washing machines, dryers, radiant room heaters (bar type fires), swimming pool equipment and floodlight/ security lights.

We should aim for water heating & pool pumps to be on off peak power supply if that is possible. If you are renting accommodation, it probably will not be appropriate to use off peak for pool pumps for two reasons: firstly, the initial cost of setting the system up and secondly, your lack of tenure and need for the landlord's approval.

Washing machines and dryers: saving will be achieved if you collect washing until you have a full load (white and colored separately) and clothes are not over spun before putting them out to dry. Even better savings will result if you use cold water washes and air dry everything.

Accurate pegging, stretching and drip drying will also save you the time and the cost of ironing in many cases. Sheets, pillow cases and table cloths are a perfect example. With more practice shirts and other garments can be dried wrinkle free. If it sounds too simple to believe, it's not; many people put a few items in the washer and set it to full load. If they set it to hot wash, even greater power is used as the machine will use heater elements to raise the water temperature to the desired level. Only use dryers if you are really forced to, not only will you be saving money but air dried clothes will smell much sweeter.

Ovens draw the most power and many modern ovens have as many as three heating elements in them. There are upper, lower and fan (back) elements. That's a whole lot of power spinning the dial on your electric meter. If you need to use the oven, use economy cooking settings and maximize cooking by consolidating all your cooking jobs so you do not have to reheat the oven day after day for different cooking jobs. Also, make sure it's turned off the minute cooking is finished. The same situation applies with the hob. In many cases you can turn the hotplate off and just let the item continue cooking on the residual heat. Where it is possible, use steamer pans for your vegetables. Not only will you save more using this method (one element instead of several) but your food will retain its colour and be more nutritious and less fattening. Don't forget to check all door seals regularly to ensure no heat loss is occurring.

Microwave cooking is fast and cost effective. It's a boon in the kitchen for various uses. I like to do microwave potatoes and rice. They are both very quick. The microwave comes into its own for fast defrosting and for reheating straight from the fridge. It's great for time challenged people and don't forget, using between 700 and 1000 watts it's about half the power used by a single element in a conventional oven.

Another way to cook without electric power is by wood fire on the family barbeque.

Fridges & Freezers: since most modern freezers are uprights and that cold air falls to the bottom and escapes, it should be obvious that the less you open the door the cheaper and more effective it will operate. Our plan here should be to add our menu items for the next day to our task list so we open the freezer once unless loading shopping into it. Planning also saves time and money by not having to defrost the freezer so often.

In the matter of the fridge, again, it's a case of the less it's opened the less coldness it will lose and therefore the cheaper it will be to run. This is a basic principle. Here are more tips to minimize running costs. Check door seals aren't leaking, don't put hot product in the fridge as it upsets gas balances (let them cool to body temperature) before you put them in the fridge. The best tip yet (worth at least $100) is if your fridge stops working and it's not caused through power loss, lay the unit on its side 24/ 48 hours so the gas balance can restore itself, then stand it upright again. Why would you pay a fridge repairman $200 plus to take your fridge for three days and do the same thing in his workshop?

Water heaters: heat store and reheat water for household use. They operate using a thermostatic sensor which determines at what temperature level the heating element restarts to heat your water. The thermostat can be adjusted and will create a saving. In any event it also serves to stop you being boiled under the shower.

FACT: the more hot water you use for baths/ showers, washing machines and cleaning the bigger your electric bill will be regardless of what tariff your supply is on.

FACT: your water heating bill will be less if your outside storage tank is lagged in thick flameproof material positioned by cable ties to minimize heat loss.

If you use a kettle, either just boil enough water for what you need or put the left over into a thermos flask which will stay hot for hours to make your next tea, coffee or soup. Boiling a full kettle for one cup is akin to standing in the street and feeding your money down the drain, coin by coin.

Power suppliers are legally allowed to perform actual meter readings only once in any twelve month period (your area may be different). The point is that half or more of your bills will be based on estimated use rather than actual use. Keep this in mind and use it to bargain down high unexpected bills. Also, don't be afraid to tell your power supplier that you want a better deal (better tariff) and that you are prepared to go to other local suppliers who are offering more bang for your buck. They know competitor rates and can usually do better for you.

Many suppliers run special programs which reward you for participation in test programs. Your cooperation allows them to control your use of power during peak demand for such items as pool pumps and air conditioners. I have been collecting $100 checks for over two years now from one company and have just successfully negotiated a discount of 10% off my total bill each quarter with my electric supplier. If you are really struggling and can do nothing else, get your supplier to set up a monthly account to make meeting the bills easier for you. Ignoring the bill or late payment will only win you a late fee penalty.

Solar Power: an asset for owner/ occupiers. Free solar power has been available for a long time but only used primarily for water heating. You just have to wonder why its use as an electric supply has taken so long. My own limited use suggests that with approximately 300 days of sun at my location per annum, it's definitely a way to go in the future. I am waiting for the data on fuel cell technology to supply power; it appears to beat everything else known at this time. With solar it's possible to sell your surplus power and therefore create a double saving after initial fees have been recovered.

Air conditioners: running units just one or two degrees lower than normal will save money.

Water. There are many ways to save water. It is important to examine your current water bill and compare it with previous bills. I learnt about saving water myself and found hundreds of tips written on this topic, for instance, "Water - Use It Wisely" website **http://tinyurl.com/ 5confc**. To be honest with you, I use at the very most 30% of these tips to conserve water. These guys suggest, "when washing dishes by hand, don't let the water run while rinsing. Fill one sink with wash water and the other with rinse water". I checked that by the time you fill the other sink with water you can rinse all your dishes with running water. What do you think? I also wouldn't use the advice on adjusting 'lawn mower blades to a higher setting'. Longer grass shades roots and holds soil moisture better than if it is closely clipped". I just don't have a lot of time (and forces) to mow my lawn very often. So when I do it, it's short. In addition, you might save water but you definitely will overspend on fuel/

electricity to run your mower more often. As I wrote before, saving is not about living in misery. It's about minimizing wasteful spending.

Internet/ Phone/ Mobile Phone/ Paid TV/ Technology

There are plenty of saving tips on all modern technology. Digital technology is rapidly becoming cheaper with time. In fact, there is something new in the marketplace everyday. Don't rush out to buy new cameras, laptops, camcorders, mobile phones or similar items. If you are willing to wait for a month or two, the same or updated product can probably be purchased just as cheaply. In addition, new doesn't necessarily mean better, but most likely will mean more expensive.

The phone is designed to make calls; it will not cook your breakfast for you, even if you pay £10,000,000.00 for it (**http://tinyurl.com/cwy6mv7**). Surprised?

Save money on your mobile phone tariff if it is possible. All my family members use the same mobile phone provider and this gives us free time to talk to each other. If you want to share just a few words with someone, texting is a cheaper option. Email and Skype are other alternatives especially if you are calling interstate or internationally. Use the plan that you really need and don't pay for extras that you wouldn't use. My mobile costs $30 per month less than my daughter's. In this case I can add another $360 of savings to my Financial Victory List.

Shop around for Internet/ home phone plans. It might be better to pay for a full package (internet, home phone, mobile phone) in order to save. With my internet package, all my local phone calls are free, so are my interstate calls. International calls are very low cost. Additionally I don't pay telephone line rental or equipment charges monthly because I run a Naked DSL system. Again, in comparison with my daughter's bills for phone/ internet I pay about $30 a month less therefore saving another $360 a year to add to my Financial Victory List.

Free and open source software is a huge area where you can save money. Have a look at the Wikipedia's list of free and open source software packages (**http://tinyurl.com/yhpfuez**).

I am sure, if you didn't dig through this list before, you will bookmark it and come back. I have been using different kind of free software for a very long time but I was honestly amazed by the amount and variety of free software tools available to us today. This book is not about software comparison. So what am I going to put into My Financial Victory List? I'll put some minimal prices for the purpose of calculation. I use free antivirus/ malware/ firewall (at least $50 yearly), plus a free CD writing/ burning software (another $30), free file compression, file sharing, file encryption, and data backup programs ($30 again). The list goes on and on and so do the savings.

I am not suggesting that you can find an alternative to every expensive software program or only to use free open source software. There are plenty of fantastic programs on the market. The question is, do you really need Adobe Photoshop or will you be happy with Adobe Photoshop Elements and its $400 price saving? Truly Adobe Photoshop does have some features that are not included in Photoshop Elements. Do you need those features or you just want to have the best? By the way, Photoshop Elements actually offers some features that are not available in Photoshop. You can download time-limited but fully functional trial versions of both programs and make your decision about buying. If you only need to edit your photographs, why not try a free image editor (for example, Gimp **http://www.gimp.org/**)?

There are endless ways to save on technology – just start doing it.

4.3. Home

Our home is the place where we can be ourselves and relax. Birds bring to their nests grass, pine needles, straw, hair, moss and feathers to make it comfortable. We build our nests in the same way. We buy comfortable furniture, appliances, clean and repair our home, pay insurance to protect everything we keep in it. We spend a lot of money to make our home more comfortable and in fact, there are a lot of possibilities to save money here.

Insurance (Home, Content)

Almost every asset can be protected by insurance, including your body parts. The art is to know what you need to cover versus what you can afford paying for it. If you own your home, you most likely need home/ contents insurance to cover you against loss or liability. Many landlords require their tenants to have building insurance coverage. There are a lot of things for you to think about and learn before you choose your level of cover, such as current house prices (re-building cost), criminal activity situation in your region, actual cash value of the goods and the replacement cost, age of your property (the condition of your plumbing, heating and electrical systems), etc. The main idea of saving on insurance is to know what you really need to cover and to properly read insurance policies before committing yourself.

If you decide to sell your house and put it on a market for let's say $550,000, the value would be x + y with the buildings valued at say $400,000 (x) and the land at $150,000 (y), then you pay insurance based on those figures. Home and contents insurance is designed to protect you against damages to the house itself, and all of your possessions in the home. If the house is destroyed by fire, lightning, windstorm, explosion, etc., the land will still be there. You only need to pay insurance for the cost of re-building and clearing the land ready to rebuild your house. Contents insurance is generally based on calculating replacing everything at new (present day) cost.

In addition, you have to be exactly sure what your insurance will and will not cover. Most insurance policies do not provide coverage for the loss due to flood, building damage by earthquake, aftershocks and mud slides, etc. Many insurance policies exempt coverage for damage caused by "Acts of God". You need to know the insurance company's definition of "Acts of God". You don't need to understand Contract law but you do need to know what coverage you have and what you are paying for. If you are paying content insurance, you have to ensure items over $1000 are declared separately, items such as jewelry, watches, stamp collections etc.

Many insurance companies will give discounts to their customers who hold other insurance policies with them such as auto or health insurance. This creates saving. Increasing your policy excesses will also save some money.

Most insurers will supply blank Assessment forms/ guides to help you calculate insurance values accurately. You will get a clear picture of your insurance needs by using these forms.

To sum up:

- Think.

- Make your decision "to have or not to have".

- Shop around and compare Policies/ prices.

- Read the fine print (what is covered by the Policy and what is not).

Home Maintenance and Repair

With home maintenance and repair the same principle applies: DIY (do-it-yourself) or pay a tradesman. Saving money on simple jobs is only limited by your imaginations and your physical abilities. I am sure you already have some basic maintenance tools like a hammer, pliers and a screwdriver (if not, get one with changeable tips), a variety of nails, screws, picture hooks, etc. It would be good to invest into drill with drill bits (suited to different surfaces), a can of WD40, for loosening screws, a tape measure, utility knife, wood saw, staple gun, a torch and inexpensive knee pads. Also, it is useful to have a vacuum cleaner, couple of spare light bulbs and a basic step ladder. The list can go on and it all depends on your circumstances and abilities.

If you plan to do some renovations and need a power paint sprayer or scaffold you might consider renting or looking for used equipment. With major repairs and home upgrades, you may be able to get a better deal if you shop for materials like tiles and paint at discount stores or warehouses.

Be careful when using handymen or trades people. Paying a handyman $15 by the hour can result in being much more expensive than paying a professional say $40 per hour. My professional guy can get the job done in two hours that takes a handyman all day.

Give a man 8 hours and he will invent ways to fill it up, especially when it's at your expense.

Household Cleaning

Most households have numerous cleaning materials many of which are extremely expensive.

Many areas of our homes can be kept clean by using a mild dish soap and plain water. Dish soap can be used as a laundry as a stain remover, a window cleaner, a surface spray, a carpet stain remover and to clean most surfaces in your home. We often turn to specialty cleaners for each different surface in our home, but dish soap is a great mild alternative that won't damage most surfaces, and manages to remove a lot of stains, dirt and grime.

A little bit of daily maintenance reduces the need for tougher cleansers to clean your home. Most stains can be removed with water, dish soap or laundry soap if they are treated quickly. Spills wiped up right away rarely need much cleanser at all to be cleaned. Make it a point to clean and maintain your home daily, and you'll find much less of a need for specialty cleaners and expensive solutions.

Store brand cleaners recently tested by TV networks showed specific low cost genetic general purpose and glass cleaners to be the best value for money.

We get stuck on the brands we know and trust a lot, but sometimes there's a store brand cleaner that works well for a fraction of the cost. As an example, the store brand of the household cleaner was forty percent less expensive than the name brand, and they are virtually identical. Look for store brands and compare ingredients. More and more store brands clean just as well as the more expensive name brands.

Our parents and grandparents cleaned windows and other sheet glass with water, vinegar and old newspapers. Vinegar cuts grease, simple as that. There are a lot of ingredients around your home that can be used to make great cleaners at a fraction of the cost. Vinegar is a great all-purpose cleaner, even the ancient Egyptians used vinegar to kill bacteria. Baking soda (Sodium bicarbonate, **http://tinyurl.com/ 6kssod**) is my favorite product; it is very versatile and helps with so many household cleaning jobs. In fact, the ancient Egyptians used natural deposits of natron, a mixture consisting mostly of sodium carbonate decahydrate, and sodium bicarbonate, as a cleansing agent like soap. It's gentle enough to use as a mild abrasive in many areas of your home. Lemons have a natural bleaching ability and also have a great grease cutting quality. If juice is added to mild soapy water, it will make an effective dishwashing liquid. Making your own cleaners can be a great way to cut cleaning costs and boost your savings.

Caution should be exercised. Avoid breathing in any fumes especially in confined spaces such as toilets.

What doesn't Kill Us Makes Us Weaker

Everybody loves the message of life relationship representation 'What doesn't kill you makes you stronger'(Friedrich Nietzsche). However, it works the opposite way in the area of many household cleaning products.

Many people use household bleach at home to whiten fabrics or remove mold/ bacteria from surfaces. It works well but household bleach is a 5% solution of a stabilized form of chlorine. Despite chlorine being added in very small amounts to some municipal water supplies when bacteria contamination threatens public health, we need to remember that chlorine is a poisonous and hazardous chemical. We may inhale chlorine by using chlorine bleach and small amounts can pass through the skin when bleach is used. Although, there is no information currently available about whether chlorine undeniably causes cancer, it definitely affects our health in a negative way. The main effects of exposure to chlorine include diseases of the lung (especially in smokers and people with breathing problems) and tooth corrosion.

Dangerous chemicals are all around us at home. My wife worked in a lab after graduating from university and accidentally burned her breathing airways with ammonia gas while working with polymer membranes. After the accident she wasn't able to continue to work with aggressive chemicals even at home. She learned a lot about dangerous (toxic) and carcinogenic chemicals which are scientifically proven to be directly involved in causing cancer. Tobacco smoke (harms you even if you don't smoke, simply because you are exposed to it), benzene, asbestos, pesticides, vinyl chloride (from which PVC is produced), perchloroethylene (a cleaning fluid, spot removers, carpet cleaners), naphthalene (mothballs) and hydrocarbons (motor fuels) have all been classified as carcinogenic. A list of dangerous chemicals can go on and on. I am not trying to scare you but you get the idea. My wife became very skilled at using nontoxic ingredients such as liquid soap, baking soda, olive oil, lemon juice and vinegar, boric acid (borax) in household cleaning/ maintenance. In addition, using all of these ingredients will save you a lot of money. So here are some of the recipes we use for home cleaning.

Furniture Polish. Ingredients: 1 cup olive oil and 1/2 cup lemon juice. Mix together in a clean spray bottle. To use, remember to shake before each application. Apply a small portion to your cleaning cloth. Spread the polish over the furniture, trying to polish evenly. Use another clean cloth to polish the dry surface. Caution: as lemon juice has a bleaching effect apply to a test area first especially on darker wood/ stain finishes.

Glass Cleaner. Ingredients: 1 cup rubbing alcohol, 1 cup water, and 1 tablespoon vinegar. Carefully mix together the three ingredients in a clean empty spray bottle. Do not reuse a spray bottle that previously had another kind of cleaner in it, since the risk of cross contamination outweighs the potential savings. You should also label the spray bottle as glass cleaner and keep it safely stored where curious pets or children will not have access. Using alcohol and white vinegar together makes a quickly evaporating glass and mirror cleaner spray that can compete with the cleaning power of big name brands. This same recipe can also be used to give a nice shine to hard tiles, chrome, and other surfaces.

My special thanks to baking soda (sodium bicarbonate), again. Whenever I stock up, I buy several boxes. It's not that baking soda can clean everything, but it can definitely make almost everything cleaner. Bicarb soda is widely used not just in baking and cleaning but in medicine, personal hygiene and many other areas. Check out these places around your home that could use a little baking soda:

- Drains. You may have seen the volcano science experiment for what happens when you pour vinegar onto baking soda. Beyond entertaining you, however, baking soda can make a huge difference in the smell and the efficiency of your drains. Try adding baking soda under hot running water to freshen the drain. Baking soda can even be used in combination with hot water to unclog a drain.

- Washing Machine. It's probably not a surprise to you that adding baking soda to a load of laundry can help freshen, and brighten clothes. Baking soda can go beyond that when used in your washing machine. It can make a great fabric softener when added to the wash (you will love the softer towels). In addition, baking soda is a great tool to actually clean your washing machine internals.

- Refrigerators. If the most you've ever done with baking soda in your refrigerator was to open a box and leave it in there, you may be missing out on some of the best benefits of using baking soda. Try sprinkling baking soda in the bottom of your crisper drawer. Baking soda can also be used to remove stains in a refrigerator. This came in quite handy when someone spilled maraschino cherry juice in the bottom of the fridge. We went from pink to pure white with a little baking soda. A small box/ dish of baking soda in the fridge will also help keep it fresh as it absorbs smells. But when it comes to deodorizing the fridge I much prefer to wipe the panels with vanilla. Yep! You read right, vanilla. It gives the whole fridge a sweet appealing smell.

• Pots and Pans. Pots and pans are my greatest challenge in the kitchen. If you have nice pots and pans, you want to be gentle enough with them to keep them looking nice, but tough enough to remove baked on food and keep them sparkling. Try using baking soda with enamel and copper pans. If you have a stained pan, baking soda does a fantastic job at removing or reducing stains. Nonstick pans that tend to absorb the odor of the food that they cook could also benefit from a baking soda soak periodically.

• Microwave Oven. Baking soda is a great tool to use when cleaning a microwave because it tackles grease, odors, and stuck on particles of food. In addition to this, baking soda can remove oily and tomato based stains. It is wonderful on the inside of the microwave and you won't have to worry about chemical residue at all.

• Ovens. Baking soda is by far the simplest oven cleaner I have found. Make sure your oven is completely cooled down before spreading a layer of baking soda in the bottom. I use a water bottle to spray the baking soda until it is damp but not saturated. Repeat every few hours and watch as the particles of food in your oven begin to dissolve.

• Dishwasher. We spend a lot of money on dishwasher detergent in an attempt to get our dishes clean. Baking soda with a little Boric Acid (borax) makes an inexpensive and highly effective homemade dishwashing detergent. What's more, adding a little baking soda to the rinse cycle of your dishwasher can help freshen the machine and remove grime and dirt inside.

Pest control. Boric Acid (borax) is a weak acid of boron and fantastic insecticide (and antiseptic). Long term exposure to boric acid may be not be the best thing for your health (don't handle it without gloves – it is a white powder/ crystals, but not sugar!) but it is not a carcinogenic substance, not toxic and used widely in medicine, makeup, oral hygiene, sunscreens and fragrances, because of its ability to limit bacterial growth. It is safe to use it in household to control cockroaches, ants, termites, fleas and silverfish.

This recipe is well-known and was used even by my grandmother. Carefully mix together a teaspoon of boric acid with five teaspoons of cheap honey (sugar will do the job but honey has a smell and attract insects better) in a glass of warm water. Soak cotton balls in this solution; put them into plastic cups/ lids and position them where you can see most ants (usually their trail). Refresh bait twice a week (no need for fresh cotton balls – just add some water to the existing baits to keep them moist). Remember, that "the more the better" doesn't work here because if you mix more boric acid in order to try to get rid of ants quicker some of the ants will die before they deliver the poisoned food to the queen and mission wouldn't be accomplished. You will eliminate a colony of ants because they take the poisoned food to the nest to feed their queen, the head of the family, and when the queen dies the whole colony dies.

Cockroaches are the most common house pests but they don't like my house. I use a simple (my own) recipe and it is much cheaper than insect sprays. I mix a teaspoon of dry weight loss cellulose powder with a teaspoon of sugar and put in places where cockroaches may live. Not far from that I put a bit of water. What do you think happens next? They eat, drink and after that die because cellulose will expand with the water. They swell and blow themselves up.

A couple of recipes for your outdoor pests. There are

plenty of recipes for homemade repellents based on garlic, onions or hot chili peppers. Mosquitoes don't like a very strong smell (neither do the people around you). I use a small 200ml spray bottle of water with a teaspoon of eucalyptus oil. Eucalyptus oil smells good, keeps mosquitoes away, and also has antibacterial effects.

White oil was used as an organic pesticide for many years and will keep your outdoor plants free of caterpillars, bugs and other leaf eaters. Simply mix together 2 tablespoons of vegetable oil with a teaspoon of cheapest dishwashing liquid in a plastic spray bottle (I use 750ml bottle). Shake until the mixture turns white; add half a liter of water and it is ready to use. Don't forget to label it! The science behind white oil is very simple. Oil and water don't mix. They separate and the oil floats above the water because it has a lower density. Dishwashing liquid is simply added as an emulsifier (to help water and oil to join together into a form called an emulsion). Thus, don't put too much dish wash liquid because an excess of it can damage some plants.

To get rid of grasshoppers with the above mixture add one clove of smashed garlic to that half a liter of water you are going to use for making white oil 24 hours (could be longer but not less) before mixing. When you are ready to use the "garlic water" strain and dispose of the garlic.

In summary, keep your home clean, uncluttered and steam-vacuumed. Save your wallet, your health and our planet.

Furniture/ Appliances

Do you remember "Need, Want and How long can it wait" List? Furniture/ Appliances definitely need careful planning for the future.

The same rules for saving money apply here:

- Set your Goals and stick to them.

- Have a look at your "Need, Want and How long can it wait" List.
- Always keep in mind that salespeople are not your friends.

Your new furniture and household appliances have a warranty and if you are not well organized with keeping your receipts together in one folder, you will ultimately have to spend your own money for repairs. So, don't forget to create your "Warranties" folder and keep you receipts there.

It seems most small electrical appliances die just after the warranty runs out. Therefore, use that knowledge to help plan your replacement appliances.

Clutter Control

Controlling clutter is a major part of keeping a house clean and home maintenance. Removing unwanted and unnecessary items from your home means you have less to clean. Less cleaning equals less cost and subsequently, more savings. The added benefit is that clutter can be turned into extra cash also through backyard sales. Getting rid of items that aren't needed will cut your cleaning time and expenses drastically. While uncluttering, you might find something you have forgotten you had! The bonus is that you will also have more time for yourself and those you love.

Go through your home contents you don't use and decide what to do with them. Some may be sold and money invested into items you really need or be added to your savings. Other items can go to charity shops to help those less fortunate than yourself (just remember a Universal Laws of Giving and Receiving: "What you give will be returned to you tenfold").

As you sow, so shall you reap.

43

4.4. Shopping

Shopping is an awful big part of the drain on family financial resources so we will cover this by breaking it down into two sections, general shopping and food shopping. Here are some things you need to know.

All smart shop owners/ managers use psychological warfare to separate you and your limited cash. In case you don't know it, lollies and toys are deliberately placed at a children's eye level because they know a child will load your basket with them and worse still, you will give in if the child throws a mini tantrum. Getting in and out is like negotiating a minefield. So if possible, shop without the kids in tow and you will spend less.

The same principles are true with convenience foods and all special items they wish to promote. Look at the shelves above and below eye level that is where you might find cheaper goods. Supermarkets often put less profitable items on bottom shelves.

Use a shopping list always and buy only what's on your list. Impulse buying destroys budgets.

Be aware that proper stock rotation of perishable foods means the items with shortest 'use by' dates are at the front. Shop owners want you to buy stock that will go out of date first or they may have to throw it away. Check the 'use by' or 'best before' dates and don't be afraid to go to the back of the shelf to get the product which will last you longer. If what you buy will be consumed the same day, there is no point to think about it.

Know which shops are promoting what specials so you can take advantage of promotions. But remember, you only win if your purchased item was on your "Need" List.

Be very careful with a "Sale of the Day" purchasing. It is a very good tool for businesses to sell their goods ("Our Sale of the Day deals can save you up to 80% off Retail Prices!"). Deals of the day can become very addictive ("Look how much I saved!" versus "Wow, how much I spent!") and can be a killer of your budget. In many cases it has been shown that false savings are promoted. In the final analysis there is no saving at all if the item bought was not planned for.

For pensioners, knowing which days your store designates as a pensioner discount day will get 5 - 10 % off your total bill.

Take reusable grocery bags with you and it will save you at least $1 a week. The majority of stores charges for plastic bags now. Just think, by saving in this way, you will help to save the planet too!

While shopping in a city, you will spend more money in shopping centers than in street shops further away. This is very simple to understand – owners of centre shops pay higher overheads than street shops due to location/ positioning. They pay higher rent, corporate fees, security fees and lighting. The increased costs are added to goods sold and the bottom line is, it comes out of your pocket.

Compare prices. We have to know prices in order to negotiate successfully.

Negotiate. Sellers often are willing to discount ("If you don't ask for a discount, you surely wouldn't get it"). They can only say yes or no. In retail, cash counts and money talks the loudest.

Generic Products

We all know by now there are plain wrap products which compete with top brand name foods. Fancy packaging, multi colour boxes and labels, huge promotional signs all cost you, as the shopper, big bucks. The cheapest printing is something like black on white and is called a two colour reverse. Black and Gold has the same cost, but five or six colour printing costs an arm and a leg and that is all passed on to you. Fancy multicolor printing adds nothing to the taste or quality of the product and ends up in the garbage bin at your expense.

Certainly not all generic products are equal to their expensive brand name neighbors. Many are and often produced by the same company on the same production line as your brand name items. When I worked as a production engineer for Ladybird Children's Clothing, the same machines at the same factory produced clothing items for Marks & Spencer's, British Home Stores (St Michael) Chilprufe, Mothercare and few others companies whose names escape me after all these years. Only the quality control and raw materials varied.

Try generic products for yourself and you will soon find which suits you and which do not. When you find what suits you, be happy watching the savings grow and you can laugh at all those filling their garbage bins with expensive printed matter.

Food/ Fruits/ Vegetables

All saving techniques we discussed previously apply here. Planning is very important to your wallet and obey math Proportional Relationships rule – the more you plan the more you save.

Meal planning is critical to your budget, your saving and your family well being. Plan meals ahead, far enough ahead that you don't need to shop so often. It's not really hard and cooking is not rocket science.

Your Family will Love you for it

By cooking at home for your family you are not only saving them from fatty takeaways, which are the cause of so much weight increase and ultimately ill health. You will be saving plenty of money and perhaps avoiding the cost of weight loss programs too.

Here's an example I shared with my single daughter who

lives in the city. I bought a joint of beef which was reduced price down to $7.99 and treated it in this manner. First, I cooked it in an oven roaster bag containing a crumbled chicken stock cube, two small cups of water and a splash of Worcester sauce. When fully cooked, the bag was opened to allow the meat to brown off. The bag juices were panned and thickened to produce delightful rich gravy. The joint was then cut partially into slices and set aside for the evening meal for two. Next, I took some meat and sliced it finely to use in a Beef and Black Bean meal with stir fry vegetables.

My next meal was Madras Curry, so I took another piece of the cooked meat and cubed it ready to add the curry ingredients which would be served with rice. You can be imaginative here. Sometimes I like just the curried meat; other times made a tropical curry in which I put sultanas, cubed apple, mango, coconut or pineapple in any combination. The great thing about curry is you can use up leftovers.

What I bought and produced served us (two adults with healthy appetites) for four main meals. The cost meat wise was $1.00 a person. If you count the stock cube, some rice, apple, sultana, black bean sauce, and stir fry chopped fresh vegetables, the total cost was less than $20.

Naturally I maximized oven use cooking several other dishes while roasting the meat and thereby effectively reducing the unit cooking cost per item cooked.

To show my daughter it was not a fluke, I repeated the cooking class using 'skin on' chicken breast which I purchased for $6.99 per kilogram. This alone saved $5 per kilogram on the normal $11.99 regular price for skinless breast chicken giving an annual saving of $260. Removal of the skin is very simple and much healthier since it contains a lot of fat.

First, I cut thin fillets which were to be cooked in a mixture of tasty spices mixed with crushed corn flakes. This makes a delicious coating, is cheap, and requires little work to achieve golden crispy coating. The thin cut meat cooks very quickly so it is also an economical method. This was later served with a light salad.

The second cut was in small strips and seasoned meat placed in enchilada wraps to create my daughter's favorite Chicken Enchiladas, which was accompanied by a spoon of sour cream, a tomato salsa, sliced, grilled capsicum and lettuce.

My next dish was a Chicken Supreme using finely shredded chicken. Make a sauce by melting butter, milk and stirring in flour until you have a smooth paste, now increase the liquid volume until it's the right consistency. Mix in the chicken and let it simmer. I like to add sliced mushrooms for taste and serve on a bed of rice.

Continuing this trend, my daughter was able to see that depending on serving size, she could get five or six good nutritious meals for $ 6.99 plus rice, salad and a couple of wraps.

All of the examples I have given lend themselves to freezing or refrigeration and once cooked will stay fresh in a proper container for 3 or 4 days minimum. I guess, most single pensioners wouldn't consider buying $8 worth of beef or a kilo of chicken but I have demonstrated using my methods that you can eat cheaper and better, cooking only once, then microwave reheating as necessary. Similarly, it is true for family units as it's all just a question of numbers. In any situation when you can buy in bulk, you will add to your annual savings.

In the case of seasonal fruits and vegetables, buy when they are at the seasonal peak supply. This is the time when usually they cost least and you can make the most savings. It's also time to make your preserves while the product is cheapest.

Simple low cost deserts are possible too. Example: jelly with small pieces of banana, peach, plums, etc. are cheap and quick. Also low cost are baked apples, semolina, apple crumble, and variations on this theme. I don't want to write a recipe book here, just to direct your line of thoughts.

Foods with a shelf life of less than two years must have a 'best before' date. Most of you will have already developed the habit of looking for the longest 'best before' date on products so that the item will last longer. It is generally safe in the majority of cases to buy produce reduced substantially because it's reached its best before date. Look carefully and make sure you don't buy tins, cartons, and cling wrapped items which are damaged or misshapen due to bloating by internal gases. Be very careful in buying fish or thawed chicken as these items can carry many bacteria, should be washed well and cooked the same day. I have never suffered problems from the use of 'Use by' or 'best before' reduced stock. I am very careful and apply a sensible approach as food hygiene is paramount.

Never refreeze thawed meat or fish. You can cook it and seal it in airtight containers to use a day or two later.

On the subject of food hygiene: it will save you money if you apply good food handling practices. Never thaw food products in warm or hot water, use cold water only. Always wash your hands first. Store items in the fridge in airtight bags or boxes, eggs keep fresher in the very bottom drawer. If you leave food items on the bench or table after use, what you are doing is reducing its life and if it's thrown out as spoiled....that's money going into the bin. Separate cutting boards should be used for meats and vegetables etc. to avoid cross contamination.

Every little action helps...look after the pennies and the dollars will look after themselves.

Other Products

Other products on your shopping list may include baby products, personal hygiene products, clothing/ shoes, cosmetics. All shopping rules we just discussed apply here. As I wrote in the beginning, saving ideas are endless. Here are some more:

- Use Coupons. I am not talking about BOGOF (Buy 1 and get 1 free) coupons. I don't advise to use these coupons unless the items from these promotions are on your "Need" List. Using BOGOF coupons actually encourages unplanned expenditure.

There are lots of discount shopper coupons or dockets around so why not put them to good use if it's for an item on your shopping list. Fuel coupons can save you when filling up the family car, so don't waste the discount which at the time of writing is anything between 4 and 22 cents per liter.

- Buy through internet/ pre-loved. Buying General Household/ Clothing items can be frustrating because sellers want to sell and, therefore, always put a positive spin on things. You are bombarded with adverts in your letter-box and on TV but not all is what it seems. If you are computer savvy, do your online research, find competitive costs, read customer feedbacks and make sure you have all the answers before you buy. Our grandmothers used to say 'act in haste, repent at leisure '.

There are some great bargains on both new and used items on Gumtree/ Craigslist and a host of other sites with the potential to save you hundreds of dollars. Similar can be found in Auction Rooms online, but you need to know what you are doing and I can't stress that enough. Even when you buy this way and pay shipping/ mailing costs you can still save.

If you need help, ask a computer savvy friend to help you if you want to buy through the internet.

- I recently saw a fabric three piece lounge suite I

know costs over $2200 sells for $400, a high end solid gold Chopard watch valued in 2004 at $8500 sells for $ 1400, a $4000 Swiss automatic coffee machine sold at just $400. A $12,000 electric Niagara Queen size bed sold for $640. Great massive savings!

• Recycling is always a great way to save. If you decided to discard your old shirt with a tear, scorch or big spot, have a look at the buttons. Sometimes buttons on old clothes may be very unusual and cost a fortune to buy. Instead of putting the shirt in a bin, cut it up for cleaning rags for those many jobs instead of using shop bought cloths. Washed ice-cream plastic boxes can be used in so many ways! Keep your bait fresh when you go fishing or your nuts and bolts organized on a shelf of your workshop. I also use them when painting.

In addition, significant savings can be made by buying from charity shops and/ or pre loved clothing shops. How far you want to take your cost cutting is a matter of individual choice. It is an area where hundreds of dollars per annum can be achieved. I know people who love shopping this way and against those who wouldn't be seen dead in a charity shop.

• Store Clearance Sales. Several stores in my city have special racks of clothes which are 25 %, 50 % and 75% off the label price. I am sure you appreciate just what you can save by being switched on. And remember, you only save if the item is on your "Need" List.

• Complain. When something you buy is not up to scratch, make management know it. As a minimum we should be looking for a fresh replacement and compensation for having to return to the store (expending our time and money for fares). Firstly, we want suppliers to lift their game. Second, we want better quality and better customer service.

If store managers don't make you happy, let them know your next complaint will be to local council health departments or to their head office. I have collected $170 in compensation for bad product in the last 3 weeks and the items were replaced too. Hold them to account, speak up, be heard and above all, assert your rights.

• Buy near to the end of the month/ quarter/ year. Many retailers will give you better discounts as they need sales to meet business projections.

We use credit card bonus points scheme which gives us $50 or $100 petrol cards to use at selected garages. My family has saved several hundred dollars a year this way.

I know what you are going to say. Why do you use credit cards if you can afford to pay cash? The answer is, it saves me carrying cash and I spend the bank's money all month long, pay off the debt balance at the end of the month and so do not pay any credit fees whatsoever. You just need to be switched on and self disciplined (this is where convenience of using credit cards comes to the game).

In summary, there are millions of sales items and therefore, it's inevitable that everything you'll ever want will come up for sale one day if not more often. Patience may be rewarded by lower cost at time of purchase.

4.5. Health

It doesn't sound right to save on health. Saving here is about wise use of your money to achieve the best outcomes for yourself and your family. When we buy a lotto ticket we want to believe that we are going to win despite mathematicians' estimation of about one in 150 million chances. When thinking about health issues we are naive, we believe that terrible health problems would never happen to us.

Just because something is in style or popular, doesn't mean it's right or good for us. Take Teflon for example, we all fell in love with Teflon. No more hard baked on dirty pans. WOW!

Since first introduced, scientists from all over the globe studied Thermal decomposition or degradation of Teflon (PTFE or polytetrafluoroethylene), which is fluorine containing polymer. There is no proof that Teflon is totally safe or unsafe for humans while using with high temperatures (frying/ boiling pans). Many cases of toxicity have been reported resulting from components of the thermal reaction. It could be a worthwhile reading Journal of Toxicology and Environmental Health about hazards in the plastics industry.

The Food and Drug Administration (FDA) instructs manufacturers to stop selling medicines that cause harm and even death. However, such products still remain on the market for months or even years before their danger is discovered. Do you remember Thalidomide (**http://tinyurl.com/s3xgn**), a sedative drug introduced in the late 1950s, which was used to treat morning sickness? It is not known exactly how many children worldwide were born with deformities. As a consequence of thalidomide use it was estimated that between 10,000 and 20,000 children were born with extreme deformities.

Recalls, Market Withdrawals, & Safety Alerts can be found on the Food and Drug Administration website **http://www.fda.gov/**.

Private Health Insurance

Without health insurance you may not be able to afford expensive medical services when you need them urgently.

Being forced to wait months, or even years on public health treatment lists can be financially devastating, especially if you are rendered unable to work. If something happened to you right now, how long could you wait to be treated in a public hospital? Usually private patients have shorter waiting periods for elective surgery. If you are young and healthy and your concerns are accidents or emergencies, you are unlikely to have a significant wait for any hospital treatment, regardless of whether you have health insurance or not, but not all treatments are free.

While comparing health insurance plans, you need to make a checklist of your own needs/ requirements and compare policies:

- The Price of the Policy: total price, payment plans/ methods, membership discounts, loyalty bonuses, treating pre-existing conditions, etc.

- Hospital Benefits: excess payment, exclusions and/ or co-payments, waiting periods, hospitals covered (public, private, physical location), private hospital emergency fees, surgery/ services (pregnancy & birth related services, infertility investigations, antenatal classes, cosmetic/ obesity surgery, digestive disorders, brain/ eyes/ heart/ knee & shoulder/ spinal fusion surgery, joint replacement, renal dialysis, rehabilitation programs, experimental treatments, accident benefits, carer accommodation in hospital/ motel in the case of the accident, and others, related to your/ your family requirements. Benefits like TV hire, phone calls, newspapers, magazines and beauty salon services could be important for some people.

- Extras Benefits: antenatal & postnatal services, dental (general, major, orthodontia), optical (single vision/ bifocals/ multifocals, contact lenses, sunglasses), complementary therapies (inclusions and overall limit) such as acupuncture, dietician, home nursing, naturopathy, physiotherapy, podiatry, psychology, remedial massage, speech therapy. Pharmaceutical prescriptions, healthier lifestyle (gym, yoga classes, weight loss programs), alternative medicines, artificial/ hearing/ other type of medically recommended aids, medical travel, and other benefits might be significant.

- Exclusions.

- Restrictions and annual limits.

You may negotiate health insurance cover with your employer. In addition, there are different regulations about public/ private health in different countries. So, you need to decide "to have or not to have your cover".

In summary, general rules applying are:

- What coverage do I/ my family need?

- Shop around and compare the services offered, rates and rebates, waiting periods for new members.

- Do not pay for what you are not going to use (for instance, I wouldn't pay for pregnancy associated services and young people wouldn't consider to pay for hip replacement surgery).

- Read the fine print (examine the cover plan to make sure that the company will pay for the things that important to you).

- Payment plans (fortnightly, monthly or annually).

Gym/ Sporting Membership

There is no doubt that exercising helps us to improve both physical and mental health. There is always the option of working out at home or outside (walking, running, bicycling) instead. We are discussing only the financial side of it. A gym membership doesn't usually come cheap (unless subscription is a part of your job benefits). A set of dumbbells, a mat and fitness games/ DVDs will not break the bank.

For some people gym/ sporting membership is a prestige issue or a place for social meetings. With others, it can be an obligation requiring self-discipline ("I paid for it, thus I must go") or time away from everyday obligations. How important is it for you?

If you decide to pay for gym/ sporting membership, think about saving on extra costs like personal training, apparel, supplements and laundry. Don't fall for "Good Deals" because salespeople at gyms will inevitably make you think these extras are unbeatable value and you can't do without them. Many gyms will offer you financial assistance because they never turn away a member who can't afford to pay.

In summary, joining a gym or a sport club will affect your wallet, so it is not a decision you should make quickly, without thinking. Signing a contract for financial assistance will be another debt for you to pay off. Debts can grow quicker than "mushrooms after the rain".

4.6. Transport

The Family Car

There is no doubt that the motorist is the most persecuted member of society. Not only do we pay huge taxes when buying our cars, especially imports, which attract 25 %. To register them, we additionally need to pay stamp duty (the second government tax) and a registration fee including third party insurance. It doesn't stop there, before the car moves we need to pay fuel tax when filling the tank. By the time the car leaves the dealers forecourt, it's lost a massive percentage of its value.

It makes good sense to buy a low kilometer used car, which can still be in spotless condition, but where someone else has paid all the big taxes and losses.

Once you have got your car, run it economically. Here is how. Don't drive short distances when you can walk…..stop/ start driving sucks up fuel. Drive reservedly, what I mean is: don't hoon, race, drive pedal to the metal or brake hard. That sucks up fuel too. Drive sedately within the signed speed limits and try to maintain the optimum economical cruising speed which was calculated to be 80 kilometers per hour or just 50 miles per hour depending on which standard is used in your country.

Real Ways to Save Fuel

There are lots of simple tips to save on fuel that cost little or nothing. Follow these ideas and a 10 - 15% fuel saving is almost guaranteed:

- Slow down. Sounds boring but true. Above about 50 mph (80 kph), driving 10% faster will use between 10 and 20% more fuel as air resistance is so much higher. Ask yourself if the time you save is worth the extra cost.

- Close windows, sunroof, and take off the roof rack to reduce air resistance/ drag. The difference is minor when empty; however, it's the small savings that can add to create the larger sum. Every little bit counts.

- Keep the air conditioning switched off unless you need it because the weather is hot or muggy (but do run it at least once a month, even in winter, to minimize compressor failure).

- Get the junk out of your trunk. Carrying excess weight wastes fuel, so think if you really need to be carrying all that heavy stuff around with you in the trunk or elsewhere.

- Anticipate. Instead of accelerating madly and then having to brake hard for junctions or traffic jams, try and anticipate the hold-up and moderate your speed so you don't need to brake so much. Braking is just throwing energy away and increasing your maintenance costs.

- Keep tyre/ tire pressures up by sticking to the recommended pressure, it will save fuel and also give better handling. Leading tyre/ tire companies advice, if your tyres/ tires are 20% under-inflated, you use up to 10% more fuel! You can get "low rolling resistance" tyres/ tires, but the extra cost may not be justified by the fuel you save. Both, under inflation and over inflation also causes wear and that increases maintenance costs. Correct inflation allows optimal performance and even wear across the tyre/ tire. If unusual wear still occurs, your steering tracking needs checking as it will most likely be out of alignment. The wheels should be balanced and rotated also.

- Use a high gear. Engines are more efficient at low speed than high speed because so much power is wasted just moving the parts of the engine. If the engine is laboring, change up a gear as we want to maintain optimal performance and therefore conserve fuel. Avoid speeds below 1500 rpm at high load. This can vary greatly between engines and vehicles.

Service

Service your car regularly; this is not so critical on modern cars. Fuel and ignition do not often go out of adjustment. It's not just the engine, if the brakes are binding slightly, this will also cause increased fuel consumption due to the increased friction.

I know it's silly, but make sure your hand-brake is fully off before you move… it will cost you money, too. You don't want to add repairs to the fuel bill by making this mistake.

In the days when the quality of fuel (petrol) has diminished and many more motorists are getting water in their fuel (for whatever reason) you can deal with that by adding one quarter cup of methylated spirit (metho, denatured alcohol) to your fuel. It will absorb all the water from fuel and do the work of high priced brand name additives produced to dispel water.

Use the correct oil. I am cautious about the various wonder additives you may see advertised. Don't use oil that is too "thin" for your engine. Consult the owner's manual and stick with the maker's recommendation or you may cause damage!

Many people have reported benefits from using cruise control, it prevents your "drifting" and, if set correctly, on long runs it helps reduce driver fatigue and the collection of speeding fines.

Check around for the best insurance prices, many insurers will allow you to pay monthly without increasing your annual premium. Obvious but needed to be stated, a good driving record will also save premiums on insurance as will agreeing a higher accident liability.

Lastly, the simple but true adage, 'Look after your car and

it will look after you'.

4.7. Education

We learn continuously from birth until we die. We learn different things and through different sources. We learn from our parents, friends, each other, from books and experiences. It is a simple formula: the more you know, the more you can do. Knowledge is power, so investing in education is a long term investment in yourself rather than source for immediate savings.

There are so many free/ discounted possibilities to further develop your educational and professional skills. For example, everyone can access Free Online Courses (**http://tinyurl.com/y7fytgq**) from Top Universities. Their collection provides a list of free educational resources for kindergarten through high school students (**http://www.ck12.org/student/**) and their parents and teachers (**http://tinyurl.com/lh3hfgn**). Also, there are links to free audio books (**http://tinyurl.com/33vazbk**), e-books (**http://tinyurl.com/yjq9nvt**), textbooks (**http://tinyurl.com/2vatcvj**); free foreign language lessons (**http://tinyurl.com/ d9lfb2x**); test prep materials (**http://tinyurl.com/kqsaur3**); and free web resources in academic subjects like literature, history, science and computing.

You can learn fee free over 300 courses, test your knowledge, and reinforce concepts through interactive exercises from Coursera website (**https://www.coursera. org**), Udacity (**https://www.udacity.com**) (Web Development course with Steve Huffman and David Evans is my favorite course there - **http://tinyurl.com/d9qleaz**). I also like free online learning tools offered by Academic Earth (**http://academicearth.org/**) and free online learning resources for basic and essential workplace skills ALISON (**http://alison.com/**).

Many organizations will happily pay for their employee's short courses (as long as they are work related). Such will save your money and give you more work opportunities for the future. Training will give you an opportunity to meet new people and expand your own network.

Also you can use promotions, free local library seminars and classes.

Big hardware stores have DIY (do it yourself) workshops to give you increased handyman skills. There are plenty of "Do-it-yourself" (DIY) videos and photos online. For example, have a look at these free DIY videos (**http://tinyurl.com/d2ov7u4**). If you learn let's say "How to install a television bracket" and do it yourself, it will save you at least $100. Google your topic of interest and you will most likely find an informed answer.

There is no doubt that you may be able to do many things, but some jobs have to be done by professionals, such as doctors, dentists, engineers, electricians and mechanics, etc. Recently I was quoted $3,500 to put two coats of paint on a 30 meter wooden fence. Would you pay that? In fact, fence painting can be a great fun to do with kids or you can organize a fence painting party. Many jobs can be fun if you want them to be!

Child Care

Child Care costs can be extremely high but saving is still possible. You need to shop around for the best prices because there are significant differences in the cost of child care and as a matter of fact, the cost is not going to show you the quality of the center.

In order to save, many parents cooperate with other parents to look after children and/ or use Community Child Care Centers. There is always a possibility to ask relatives/ grandparents to help or "energy exchange" (offering some of your skills/ time in exchange for looking after your child).

Also, you can offer some of your skills to a child care in order to reduce your costs (accounting, cleaning, lawn mowing, handyman/ repair). Some employers can help with costs and there is some government help available in many countries. Explore church and charitable support programs. Working from home or combination of flexible hours and babysitter might help.

School/ College Fees

Education doesn't come cheap. Private education is even more expensive. Many parents are going through a dilemma about choosing a private or public school? Which is better? How can you compare private and public schools? There are many factors involved in consideration such as facilities, budgets, class size, teaching, administrative support, etc. Some parents come from saying "You get what you paid for" and assume that private schools offer superior education. Others contend that public schools provide more real-life experiences. I am not advocating for either and it is your decision to make. There is the question to ask yourself when you are making your decision about a school, "Is it about your child's future, your ego and prestige or child's academic success?" My children studied only in public schools. The oldest daughter works in a hospital as a psychologist and the youngest just completed her PhD in Science from the best university in our state and received the Dean's Award for her achievements.

There are some ways to save here such as applying for scholarships or relocating to the area closer to the chosen study center.

If your child's academic success is important to you, you can help your children to manage their study and development. Reading a bedtime story to your child is a form of child development and great way of bonding!
Make learning fun by playing educational games with kids.

Some examples:
Interactive Maths Games (**http://www.learningplanet. com** - **http://tinyurl.com/n3hwem**),
Maths Is Fun (**http://www.mathsisfun.com**/),
Games and Activities (**http://www.cut-the-knot.org**/),
Simply Science (**http://tinyurl.com/d5sed6w**),
English Language (**http://tinyurl.com/yf9xdux**),
Educational Word Games (**http://tinyurl.com/ n6bjwj2**).
The list can go on. Just Google what you need to search for and you will get plenty of learning websites/ blogs options which will help your kids with learning and save your money on tutoring.

Your Upskilling

By definition, upskilling is the improving of aptitude for work by a person through additional training. For instance, enrolling into a course at a higher level than any course you have completed previously is, therefore, upgrading your skills.

The recruitment world is competitive. Improvement/ expansion of your existing skills and developing new ones are always a win-win situation for everyone. This can lead to a higher paid/ more interesting/ more secure job.

There are some government funded courses/ incentives (online or by correspondence) in many countries. These are available to fund or subsidize upskilling of existing workers, new employees, unemployed people, mature age workers (aged 50 years and over) and women returning to work, etc.

Saving is not about putting coins into the piggy bank. Saving is about planning and thinking. Investing finances into your own upskilling pays for itself many times over. So, plan, think, learn, and grow.

4.8. Entertainment

We all want to save money, but we still want to have a life. The decision to save money is like a stop smoking decision. Most people know they have to do it, but few have the willpower to get the job done. We want to save on our bills but not to lose out on the entertainment. Why not consider a candle light dinner at home instead of the $ 100 plus dinner at some swish club? A night at home with a rental DVD will do the trick for a few dollars as opposed to a night at the movies costing $30 -$40 taking food and drinks into account. Don't shoot me on the numbers, these are just examples. The idea I am conveying to you is that you don't need to become too severe and halt all entertainment.

Having a Great Time

Entertainment covers most of our free time and pleasures: Movies/ Theater/ Shows/ Music, Newspapers/ Magazines, Bars/ Clubs/ Alcohol/ Cigarettes, Celebrations, Hobbies, Holidays and Eating out.

There are plenty of ways to save on entertainment and still have a great time. Get creative and you will see many cheap and free entertainment options for you, your family and kids. If your idea of fun is a good meal, then consider staying in, cooking and may be inviting friends over to watch a DVD. Have a karaoke night, a fancy dress or pajama party, a treasure hunt or horoscope reading. Do you remember the fence painting party? You can host a game night to play some old fashioned board games or experiment with makeup or hair color, have a bubble blowing contest or learn line dancing, plan a fundraising event or a trip, go roller skating or fishing, start a new hobby, learn a new language. Theme parties are great, for example, "around the world": choose a country of the world, prepare decorations, choose costumes, learn some phrases, and cook the native food unique to that country. If you video record this party, watching the video can be an idea for the next party. Start cartooning online, create paper snow flakes or origami – the list can go on and is limited only by your imagination. So don't put too much stress on your wallet. Be a creative thinker. You will be surprised at how much fun you can have while saving.

You will save heaps of money by taking prepared food with you to work for lunch (for yourself, partner and kids). I'm not talking necessarily about sandwiches, but salads are so easy to make. You know the difference in the price of an apple in a supermarket and one in the café. What we eat out costs us as a minimum 100% more for the same meal prepared at home, so you will save at least that amount in a day.

It wouldn't be very hard to save on such things as chips and cakes in your lunch break, or magazines, DVDs and chewing gum, etc. Most of the snacks have no benefit to your health and magazines/ DVDs you can borrow from friends or your local library.

By cutting on buying soft drinks and through filling bottles at home with filtered (or cold boiled) water, you can only benefit. You gain weight from soft drinks and worse still, you may later have to spend money on weight loss/ dental programs. Just replace fizzy drinks with water which is better for you anyway. If you start to add a slice of lemon, orange or lime to your water, it will boost your body immune system with vitamin C and later you might avoid the costs of anti-flu medication.

Here is an example of calculating:

- By not buying:
1 magazine a month = $5 x 12 = $60 saving a year;
a pack of unhealthy chips a week = $3 x 52 = $156 saving a year;
a couple of soft drinks a week = $3 x 52 = $156 saving a year;
a cup of coffee a day = $3 x 365 = $1095 saving a

year.

- Saving:
$10 on cigarettes a week = $10 x 52 = $520 saving a year;
$5 on alcohol drink a week = $5 x 52 = $260 saving a year;
$25 on lunches, that you made at home and didn't buy from a cafe a week = $25 x 52 = $1300 saving a year.

So, here is $3547 in annual saving (not to mention other saving) on things that you really can do without. Will it be enough for a holiday? Will it pay off your credit card? Will it take some stress off you?

Gifts

It's important while considering gifts to think what kind of gift will make the person happy. Giving an expensive gift can make anyone feel uncomfortable. Recycling gifts might be possible but there is a probability it could make the recipient very unhappy. One of my wife's friends gave her a very nicely wrapped box of handcrafted Halloween candles for Christmas. My wife was quite upset as you can imagine.

If you have a crafting hobby, consider integrating that into your gift (hand knitted warm socks might be really great gift) or create a nice fruit basket (wouldn't break the bank and healthy), consider Gift Certificates or just Google for ideas.

Visitors

Some visitors/ guests at your home can put plenty of financial strain on your budget. Sometimes it doesn't feel you are being polite if you tell your visitors about it. You have no choice but to learn how to do it and be honest with your guests and yourself. You may need to tell them that currently you are living on a limited budget and can't afford certain things. Being honest doesn't mean being rude or creating a conflict. Being unhappy will be a source of anger for you, may later cause disagreements and distant relationships. Just keep in mind that it's important to remain respectful of the other person.

Gambling/ Lotto

Every one of us wants to know how to increase our chances of winning the lottery. Many authors claimed that they created a method that he/ she and members of their family use that has enabled them to WIN several lottery GRAND prizes. Each one of them claims that their method is the best, very easy to use and will work with any type lottery games (scratch tickets or number games) in any state or country. Did you ever ask yourself a simple question – why do they offer their method? If they know how to win and have been winning lottery games, why do they bother to write about it? Instead, they should be having a good time at the most expensive beach resorts, spending their GRAND prize money while driving their new Rolls Royce. Is it that they are just so kind and want everybody to be a GRAND prize millionaire? There is luck; there are lucky days in our life, and I believe that magic does happen, but not because we try to learn someone else's system of winning numbers. Do I really need to say it? Buy their system and you are helping to make them millionaires.

Some people try to prove that buying more tickets does not increase your odds. Others try to prove the completely opposite. From our brain's logic we believe that buying more lottery tickets definitely increases our chances to win. On the other hand, by using a function in statistics called Poisson distribution (**http://tinyurl.com/9zg9d**), one can prove that the more lotto tickets you buy the least chance of winning you have.

You heed to remember that gambling (buying lotto tickets, playing poker, slot machines, or roulette, sport bets or internet gambling) is addictive and are a mental health problem. It destroys families and lives.

5 ARE YOU READY TO BEAT MY FINANCIAL VICTORY LIST?

Let's start today!

My Financial Victory List (from calculations used in a book):

- By not buying:
1 magazine a month = $5 x 12 = **$60** saving a year;
2 packs of unhealthy chips a week = $6 x 52 = **$312** saving a year;
3 soft drinks a week = $9 x 52 = **$468** saving a year;
a cup of coffee a day = $3 x 365 = **$1095** saving a year.

- Saving:
$5 on alcohol drink a week = $5 x 52 = **$260** saving a year;
$25 on lunches, that you made at home and didn't buy from a cafe a week = $25 x 52 = **$1300** saving a year;

$2 on bottle of water (filled from home, 5 days a week) = $10 x 52 = **$520** saving a year;
$10 on car wash (as I still use my water and a car shampoo) a week = $10 x 52 = **$520** saving a year.

- Saving on Technology (see 4.2):
Mobile phone cost = $30 x 12 = **$360** saving a year;
Home/ mobile Internet cost: = $30 x 12 = **$360** saving a year;
Using some free software = **$150** saving a year (at least).

- Saving on Utilities (see 4.2):
Switching off lights and appliances when not actually in use = $15 x 12 = **$180** saving a year;
Consolidating most cooking jobs: = $50 x 12 = **$600** saving a year;
Consolidating washing: = $20 x 12 = **$240** saving a year.

- Saving on Insurance:
(Home, Content) (see 4.3):
Finding best deal and negotiating: = $25 x 12 = **$300** saving a year;
Car insurance (see 4.7):
Finding best deal and negotiating: = $20 x 12 = **$240** saving a year.

- Saving on Household Cleaning (see 4.3):
Using just vinegar and soda for cleaning (saving a planet, too!) = $10 x 12 = **$120** saving a year;
Home made insecticide, pesticides, repellents = $20 x 12 = **$240** saving a year.

- Saving on groceries (see 4.4):
Buying 'skin on' chicken breast = $10 x 52 = **$520**

saving a year;
Buying meat/ fish in small bulk packs = $10 x 52 = **$520** saving a year;
Buying fruits/ vegetables in season in small bulk = $10 x 52 = **$520** saving a year;
Reusable grocery bags = $1 x 52 = **$52** saving a year.

- Other shopping
Generic Brand name toiletries (face moisturizer: = $10 x 12, toothpaste: = $10 x 12, deodorant, soap, shampoo, conditioner, shower gel, etc) = $40 x 12 = **$480** saving a year.

- Health
Private Health Insurance: = $50 x 12 = **$600** saving a year.

So, here is my $**10,017.00** annual saving.

I didn't calculate savings from smoking as I don't smoke. Or I didn't put in my Financial Victory List savings from dying my hair at home as I don't dye my hair (but my daughter told me that dying her hair by herself saves her about $100 in three months, which is $400 saving a year).

So, now it is you turn to create YOUR Financial Victory List!
I would like to conclude by saying that I'm grateful for having an opportunity to share my thoughts, knowledge and experience with you.
Now it's all about YOU! Just start the first day of the rest of your life!
Good luck and I hope to hear from you. Thank you for purchasing this book.

Lawrence Burns

APPENDIX

Useful Online resources:

* Wikipedia website:
Comparison of spreadsheet software
http://en.wikipedia.org/wiki/Comparison_of_spread
sheets

Debt-snowball method
http://en.wikipedia.org/wiki/Debt-snowball_method

List of free and open source software packages
http://en.wikipedia.org/wiki/List_of_free_and_open
_source_software_packages

* Australian Securities and Investments
Commission's (ASIC) consumer website MoneySmart
https://www.moneysmart.gov.au/

- Calculators:

Credit Card Repayment Calculator
http://www.creditcards.com/calculators

Finance calculators
http://www.thecalculatorsite.com/finance/

Health calculators
http://www.thecalculatorsite.com/health/

- U.S. Department of Energy http://energy.gov

- Water Use It Wisely
http://www.wateruseitwisely.com/

- U.S. Food and Drug Administration
http://www.fda.gov/

- Education:

Free Online Courses
http://www.openculture.com/freeonlinecourses

CK-12 Foundation http://www.ck12.org/student/

WatchKnowLearn http://www.watchknowlearn.org/

Coursera https://www.coursera.org/

Udacity https://www.udacity.com/

Class Central http://www.class-central.com/

Academic Earth http://academicearth.org/
.

- Educational games with kids:

Pearson Education (Family Education Network)
http://www.funbrain.com/ ,
http://www.infoplease.com/

Interactive Maths Games (LearningPlanet)
http://www.learningplanet.com/stu/index.asp

Maths Is Fun http://www.mathsisfun.com/

Games and Activities Cut the knot http://www.cut-the-knot.org/

The Simply Science Site
http://users.pipeline.com.au/~jpearce/default.htm

English Language
http://www.digitaldialects.com/English.htm

Educational Games
http://www.learninggamesforkids.com/

Learning Games for Kids
http://www.thekidzpage.com/learninggames/

- Upskilling

ALISON (Advance Learning Interactive Systems
Online) http://alison.com/

Open Education Database http://oedb.org/open/

Free Computer Tutorials
http://www.gcflearnfree.org/computers

Free Typing Tutor & Typing Test

http://www.learn2type.com/

- Do it Yourself

Do It Yourself Network
http://www.diynetwork.com/

Do It Yourself Appliance Repair
http://www.appliancerepair.net/

Do It Yourself Ideas http://www.bhg.com/
decorating/do-it-yourself/

Bunnings (Do It Yourself videos)
http://www.bunnings.com.au/learn-how-to-
DIY_diy-videos.aspx

Better Homes and Gardens (Do It Yourself videos)
http://www.bhg.com/videos/video-index

Handy man projects http://www.hammerzone.com/

Hometime's How-To Center
http://www.hometime.com

Walls project needs http://www.drywalltips.org/

INDEX

U

Upskilling
   defined, 63
   investing into your future, 63
Utilities
   defined, 13
   saving tips, 26

V

Victory Saving Program
   importance, 23
Visitors, 66

W

Water
   ways to save, 30

My NEED List:

I Need	How Long Can it Wait

My WANT List:

I Want	How Long Can it Wait

My Victory List

№	Item	Saving

www.ingramcontent.com/pod-product-compliance
Lightning Source LLC
Chambersburg PA
CBHW051341170526
45166CB00002B/909